BONUS

Want a Bonus?

Download The Vision Board Freebie:
5 Steps to Create a Vision Board that Works E-Book
&
Vision Board Goal Setting Workbook
Link: bit.ly/vision_board_freebie

60 Positive Affirmation cards + 30 Inspirational quote cards For Vision Boards

60 Positive Affirmation cards + 30 Inspirational quote cards For Your Vision Board

DOWNLOAD

Link: bit.ly/affirmations-quotes-cards

Or Use QR Code

FOLLOW US

Instagram QR Code

MANIFESTHAPPINESSCHANNEL

Follow Us On Instagram: @manifesthappinesschannel
Subscribe to Our Youtube Channel:
youtube.com/c/manifesthappinesschannel

For More Vision Board Clip Art Books
Visit Our Page on AMAZON

Link: bit.ly/mh_press

or Use QR Code

We Have Vision Board Clip Art Books For :

Women, Men, Teens, Kids, Travel, Self-love, Weight Loss, Wedding, Word Art, Health, Affirmations, Vision Board Parties, Business & Money and more

Money

ABUNDANCE

$100,000

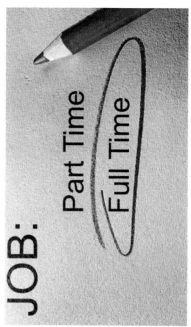

Got Promoted

PROMOTION

SALARY UP

SALARY INCREASE

JUST AHEAD

Start Up

Entrepreneur

Small business owner

CEO

Multiple Income Streams

Debt Free
Just Ahead

ABUNDANCE

freedom

Freedom

Debt Free

WEALTH

Rich

to be best in
point of vie
Rich
great ort
posses
wealth,

Buying

Shopping

Luxury

Dream Car

Dream House

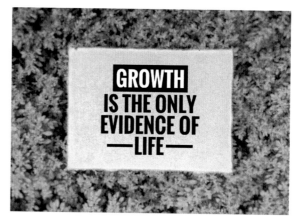

Real Estate

SPEND

SAVE

INVEST

nvest

CERTIFIED

CAREER →

Success

CAREER
PATH
AHEAD

Prosperity

Travel The World

Made in the USA
Las Vegas, NV
28 November 2024

12853148R00024